Scholastic Success With
Reading Comprehension

Grade 2

by Robin Wolfe

SCHOLASTIC
PROFESSIONAL BOOKS

New York • Toronto • London • Auckland • Sydney •
Mexico City • New Delhi • Hong Kong • Buenos Aires

Cover art by Victoria Raymond
Cover design by Maria Lilja
Interior illustrations by Mark Mason
Interior design by Quack & Company

ISBN 0-439-44490-X

12   40   09

Scholastic Professional Books

Introduction

Parents and teachers alike will find **Reading Comprehension** to be a valuable learning tool. Children will enjoy reading a wide variety of stories that are humorous or informative. The activities include puzzles, brain teasers, and fun ways of finding answers and are tools for improving comprehension skills. Finding the main idea, reading for details, drawing conclusions, and following directions are just some of the skills included. Second graders are also challenged to develop vocabulary, identify cause and effect, and analyze characters. They are encouraged to try different reading strategies that will help them become better readers. Take a look at the Table of Contents. You will feel rewarded providing such a valuable resource for your children.

Remember to praise children for their efforts and successes!

Table of Contents

Scholastic Professional Books

Try This!

*When you are reading, do you get stuck on words that you don't know? Does not knowing a word make it hard to understand what you are reading? This idea can help you. Use **context clues** to figure out what the word is. That means think about the other words in the sentence. What clues do they give? Then ask yourself what other word would make sense there.*

What do you think the underlined word means in each sentence below? Circle the meaning that makes sense. Then rewrite each sentence using the meaning instead of the underlined word.

1. My domino has two white <u>pips</u>, and yours has five.

   baby dogs   spots   long metal tubes

   _____

2. A gray <u>fulmar</u> flew by the cruise ship.

   lizard   swordfish   seabird

   _____

3. The queen had a beautiful necklace made of <u>jasper</u>.

   a green stone   yellow pudding   wet snow

   _____

4. My sister is the best <u>flutist</u> in the high school band.

   waitress   runner   flute player

   _____

Write a meaning for this nonsense word: zeebit. Use it in a sentence on another piece of paper. See if a friend can guess the meaning of your word by looking at the clues in the sentence.

Moon Walk

➡️ *The **main idea** tells what the whole story is about.*

Neil Armstrong was an astronaut. He made history on July 20, 1969. He was the first man to walk on the moon! When he stepped on the moon, he said, "That's one small step for (a) man, one giant leap for mankind." Millions of people were watching this amazing event on TV. It was an awesome thing to look up at the moon that night and know that a man was walking around on it! For years, people had wondered if there would be moon creatures living there. But the only things Armstrong found were moon rocks and moon dust.

Draw a line connecting the correct star words that tell the main idea of the story. Begin at Earth. Some star words will not be used.

uncle ☆   dance ☆   walk ☆   moon 🌕

to ☆

river ☆   cold ☆   uncle ☆   on ☆

the ☆

Armstrong ☆   was ☆   man ☆

frog ☆

Neil 🌍   hat ☆

the ☆   plate ☆   candy ☆

first ☆

💡 **Write a short story with this title: "My Trip to the Moon." Underline the main idea of the story.**

ABC

*The **main idea** of a story tells what the whole story is about.*

When you were in kindergarten, or maybe before that, you learned your ABCs. Letters are the building blocks for words. Words are the building blocks for sentences. We use sentences to communicate our thoughts and feelings. Each letter of the alphabet has at least one sound. Some letters have more than one sound. There are 26 letters in our alphabet. Many of our letters came from alphabets made many years ago in foreign countries. In fact, the word *alphabet* comes from two words, *alpha* and *beta*, which are the first two letters in the Greek alphabet!

Underline the title that describes the main idea of this story.

Playing With Blocks   All About Our Alphabet   The Greek Language

Now let's play a game using the alphabet. Read each clue below. Draw a line to the letters that sound like the correct answer.

1. I borrowed some money from your piggy bank. _____ fifty cents.

2. This math is not hard. It's _____.

3. What did the blind man say to the doctor who made him see again? _____

4. What insect makes honey? _____

5. What a Plains Indian used to sleep in? _____

6. I drank all my milk. Now my glass is _____.

7. What kind of plant is that? _____

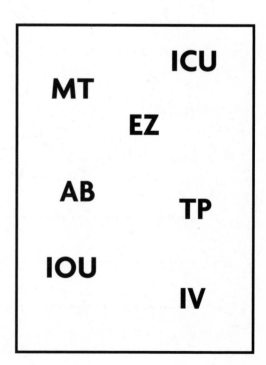

ICU

MT

EZ

AB

TP

IOU

IV

Scholastic Professional Books

Call the Police!

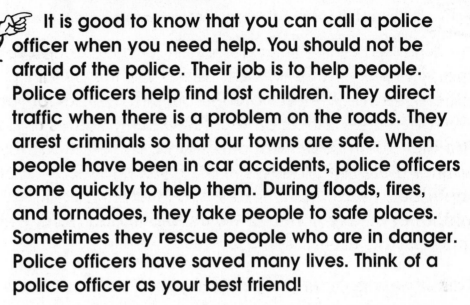

It is good to know that you can call a police officer when you need help. You should not be afraid of the police. Their job is to help people. Police officers help find lost children. They direct traffic when there is a problem on the roads. They arrest criminals so that our towns are safe. When people have been in car accidents, police officers come quickly to help them. During floods, fires, and tornadoes, they take people to safe places. Sometimes they rescue people who are in danger. Police officers have saved many lives. Think of a police officer as your best friend!

What do you think the main idea of this story is? To find out, read the letters that are connected in the puzzle. Write the letters in order beside the matching shapes.

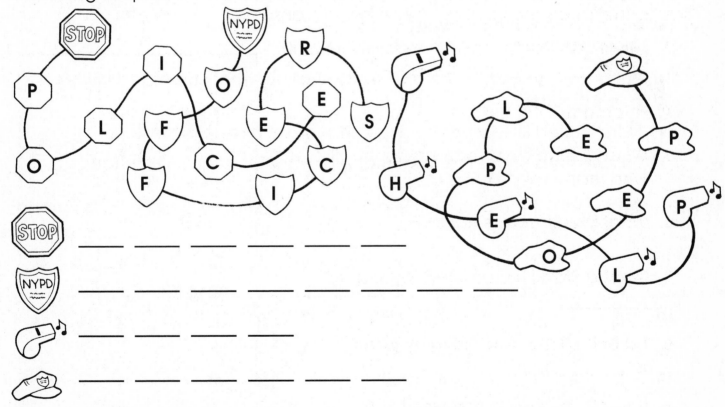

_ _ _ _ _ _ _ _ _ _

_ _ _ _ _ _ _ _ _ _

_ _ _ _

_ _ _ _ _ _ _

 Write a letter to your town's police officers. Make sure the letter's main idea is to thank them for keeping your town safe. Ask an adult to mail it for you.

Rachel's Recipe

 Details *are parts of a story. Details help you understand what the story is about.*

On Saturday, Rachel got up early. Her mom was still asleep, so Rachel made her own breakfast. She put some peanut butter in a bowl. She mixed it with a little honey. Then she stirred in some oatmeal, bran flakes, and raisins. It tasted yummy! When Mom got up, she said, "Oh! You made granola!"

Follow the directions below.

- **Circle the word that tells who the main character is.**

- **Underline the word that tells what day Rachel made breakfast.**

- **Put a box around the word that tells what dish Rachel put the peanut butter in.**

- **Put a star by each of the four words that tell what she mixed with the peanut butter.**

- **Put a dotted line under the word that describes how it tasted.**

- **Put two lines under the word that tells what Mom called the food.**

Now find each of the nine words in the puzzle below and circle it. The words go across and down.

B	R	A	N	F	L	A	K	E	S	M	H	N	C	L
O	A	T	M	E	A	L	B	K	E	Q	O	J	W	I
W	R	A	I	S	I	N	S	G	R	A	N	O	L	A
L	G	S	A	T	U	R	D	A	Y	P	E	R	D	R
G	R	A	C	H	E	L	Y	U	M	M	Y	F	A	H

 On another sheet of paper, draw your favorite breakfast. Then write the steps to prepare it.

Scholastic Professional Books

Rodeo Clowns

➡️ **Details** *are parts of a story. Details help you understand what the story is about.*

Have you ever been to a rodeo or seen one on TV? If so, you probably saw some rodeo clowns. Like clowns at a circus, they entertain the audience by doing funny tricks to make people laugh. But the main job of rodeo clowns is to protect the cowboys from the bulls. They try to catch the bull's attention long enough to allow the cowboy to escape from the arena without getting hurt. Bulls are quite fast, and they make sudden moves, so it is hard to get away from them. Angry bulls use their horns as weapons. Rodeo clowns sometimes jump in a barrel while the bull pushes it around. Other times they wave their arms or yell to keep the bull away from the cowboy. They make it look like a funny game, but it is really a very dangerous job.

Circle the letter under true or false to show your answer.

True	False	
B	Z	1. Rodeo clowns do funny tricks.
R	U	2. Rodeo clowns work at the circus.
L	M	3. Rodeo clowns help protect the cowboys.
A	L	4. Rodeo clowns distract the goats while the cowboy gets away.
R	X	5. Rodeo clowns are brave.
I	V	6. Bulls can make sudden moves.
F	D	7. Bulls use their tails as weapons.
P	E	8. Sometimes rodeo clowns jump in a cardboard box while the bull pushes it around.
R	W	9. Sometimes rodeo clowns yell and wave their arms to distract the bulls.
S	C	10. Rodeo clowns have a very dangerous job.

To find out who likes rodeo clowns, write the letters you circled in order.

___ ___ ___ ___ ___ ___ ___ ___ ___ ___

Gorillas

Details *are parts of a story. Details help you understand what the story is about.*

Gorillas are the largest apes. They live in the rain forests of Africa. Every morning, they wake up and eat a breakfast of leaves, fruit, and bark. During most of the day, the adult gorillas take naps. Meanwhile, young gorillas play. They wrestle and chase each other. They swing on vines. When the adults wake up, everyone eats again. When there is danger, gorillas stand up on their hind legs, scream, and beat their chests. Every night before it gets dark, the gorillas build a new nest to sleep in. They break off leafy branches to make their beds, either on the ground or in the trees. Baby gorillas snuggle up to their mothers to sleep.

Find the answers to the puzzle in the story. Write the answers in the squares with the matching numbers.

Across

1. During the day, adult gorillas _____.

3. Gorillas eat leaves, bark, and _____.

5. The largest apes are _____.

7. In danger, gorillas beat their _____.

8. Young gorillas swing on _____.

Down

2. The continent where gorillas live is _____.

4. When young gorillas play, they _____ and chase each other.

6. Baby gorillas snuggle up to their mothers to _____.

On another piece of paper, write two things gorillas do that people also do.

Scholastic Professional Books

Fun at the Farm

 Story events that can really happen are **real**. *Story events that are make-believe are* **fantasy**.

Read each sentence below. If it could be real, color the picture. If it is make-believe, put an X on the picture.

 Dairy cows give milk.

 **The farmer planted pizza and hamburgers.**

 **The pig said,"Let's go to the dance tonight!"**

 **The mouse ate the dinner table.**

 **The hay was stacked in the barn.**

 **The chickens laid golden eggs.**

 The green tractor ran out of gas.

 The newborn calf walked with wobbly legs.

 **The goat and the sheep got married by the big tree.**

 Two crickets sang "Mary Had a Little Lamb."

 Horses sat on the couch and watched TV.

 **Rain made the roads muddy.**

 **Four little ducks swam in the pond.**

 **The farmer's wife baked a pumpkin pie.**

 On another sheet of paper, write one make-believe sentence about the farmer's house and one real sentence about it.

Grandma Hugfuzzy

Grandma Hugfuzzy lived all alone in the country. She loved to sit on the porch and watch the animals. Every day, she put food out for the rabbits and raccoons. She fed the birds with scraps of bread. She put corn out for the deer. One terrible, awful, dreadful day, Grandma Hugfuzzy's house burned down. Poor Grandma! She had nowhere to go and no one to help her. She spent the night in an old barn on a bed of hay, crying herself to sleep. During the night, the animals came to her rescue. Nine black bears chopped down some trees. A herd of deer carried the wood on their antlers. Dozens of raccoons and squirrels worked all night building a log cabin for Grandma. Birds flew above the house nailing on the roof. When morning came, Grandma Hugfuzzy was amazed to see what her animal friends had done! She threw a big party for them that lasted ten years!

Write a red *R* on things that are real. Write a purple *F* on things that are fantasy.

a woman feeding animals

deer that carry lumber

a grandmother living alone

sleeping on hay in a barn

animals building a log cabin

Home Sweet Home

WELCOME

a house burning down

bears chopping down trees

birds that can nail on a roof

crying that her house burned

a party that lasted ten years

 The first part of this story could be real. Draw a big orange star at the place where the story changes to fantasy.

Scholastic Professional Books

The Change Game

Each sentence below is make-believe. Change it!
Rewrite the sentence so that it is real.
Study the example.

The broom carried the dog to the moon.

The broom was kept in the closet.

1. The newborn baby was bigger than a house.

_____

2. The walls were painted with gooey green slime.

_____

3. The Queen of England turned into a frog.

_____

Now change and do it the other way! Each sentence below is real.
Change it so that it is fantasy. Study the example.

The moon is made of rocks and ice.

The moon is made of green cheese.

4. The black spider crawled across the floor.

_____

5. The deep-sea diver saw a whale and five dolphins.

_____

6. My pizza has pepperoni and olives on it.

 _____

On another piece of paper, draw a picture about one of your fantasy sentences.

The Rescue

 Sequencing *means putting the events in a story in the order that they happened.*

Mia's black cat climbed to the top of a telephone pole and couldn't get down. "Come down, Spooky!" cried Mia. Mia thought hard. What could she do? She went across the street to ask Mr. Carson for help. He was a firefighter before he retired. "What's the matter, Mia?" asked Mr. Carson when he saw Mia's tears. "My cat is up on that pole, and I can't get her down!" Mr. Carson hugged Mia and said, "I'll call my buddies at the fire station. They will come and help." A few minutes later, Mia saw the fire truck coming. The firefighters parked near the pole and raised a long ladder to the top. A firefighter climbed the ladder and reached out for Spooky. Just then, Spooky jumped to a nearby tree limb, climbed down the tree, and ran into the backyard. Mia said, "Spooky! You naughty cat!" Mr. Carson and the firefighters laughed and laughed.

Read the sentences on the ladder. Number them in the order that they happen in the story.

Mia asked Mr. Carson for help.

Mr. Carson called his firefighter friends.

The firefighters laughed.

A firefighter climbed the ladder.

Mia begged Spooky to come down.

Spooky jumped to a tree and climbed down.

The fire truck came.

Mia scolded Spooky.

New Kid in School

When they finished moving, Mom took Shelby to meet her new teacher. The teacher said, "Welcome to our school, Shelby. Let me tell you what we do in our second-grade class. We start the day with reading and writing. After that, we do math. Then we go out to recess. Just before lunch, we have social studies. We eat lunch at 11:00. Then we have story time. After story time, we have science. Then comes learning centers, where you can work on the computer, play a game, or read a book. Next, we have spelling. Finally, we go to music and art classes for the last hour of the day. Here is a schedule for you to take home. I'll see you tomorrow, Shelby!"

Fill in the blanks with the missing words or time.

Second-Grade Class Schedule

8:00	Reading and _____
9:00	_____
10:00	_____
10:30	_____
__:__	Lunch
11:30	_____
12:00	_____
1:00	Learning Centers
1:30	_____
2:00	_____ and Art
3:00	Go home.

A Pencil Sandwich?

How does the lead get inside a wooden pencil? Pencils are made out of strips of wood cut from cedar trees. Then grooves are cut in the strips. Graphite is laid into the grooves. (We call it lead, but it is really graphite.) Then another strip of wood is glued on top of the first one, making a pencil sandwich! The wood is rounded in rows on the top strip of wood and the bottom strip. Then the pencils are cut apart and painted. An eraser is added on the end and held in place by a metal ring. When you buy a pencil, you sharpen it, and then you are ready to write.

Look at the pictures. Number them in the order that they happen in the story.

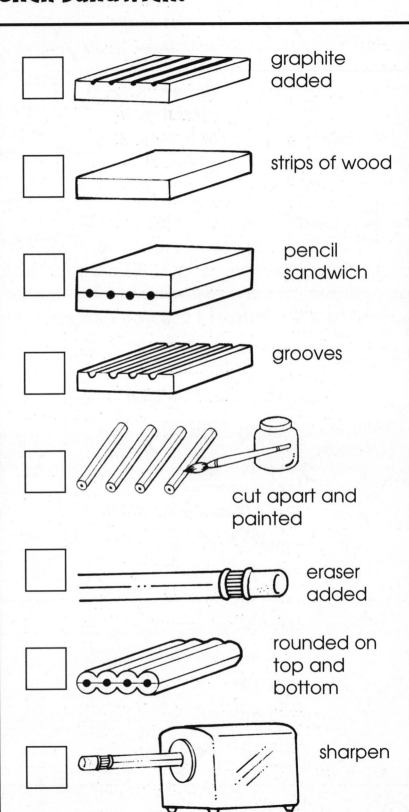

graphite added

strips of wood

pencil sandwich

grooves

cut apart and painted

eraser added

rounded on top and bottom

sharpen

 Use a pencil to practice writing the alphabet, uppercase and lowercase.

Secret Message

Follow the directions in each shape. Write the answer in the shape that matches it. If you follow directions carefully, you will discover a secret message!

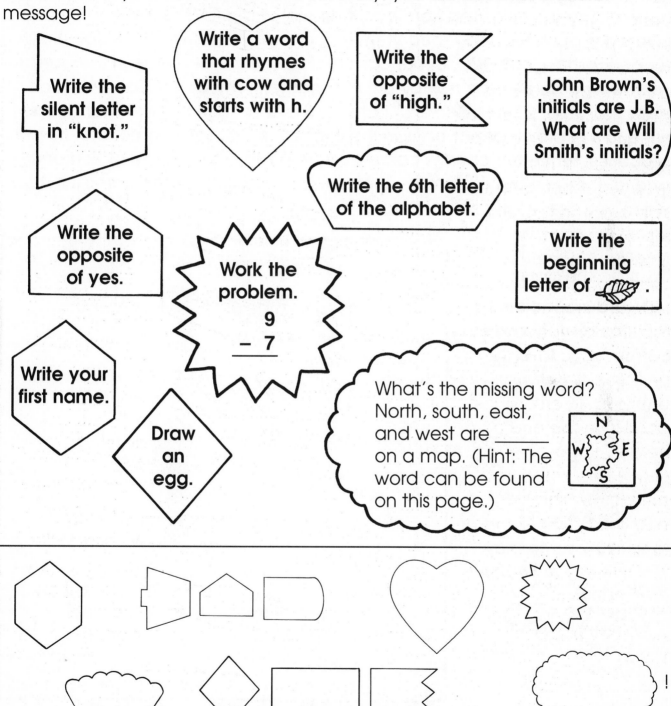

Write the silent letter in "knot."

Write a word that rhymes with cow and starts with h.

Write the opposite of "high."

John Brown's initials are J.B. What are Will Smith's initials?

Write the 6th letter of the alphabet.

Write the opposite of yes.

Work the problem.
9
− 7

Write the beginning letter of 🍂.

Write your first name.

Draw an egg.

What's the missing word? North, south, east, and west are _____ on a map. (Hint: The word can be found on this page.)

 Write step-by-step directions that tell how to make a peanut butter and jelly sandwich.

Rainy Day Fun

One rainy afternoon, Sharon and I decided to play grocery store. We went to the garage and set up four empty boxes for our shelves. Mom let us have all the canned food from the pantry to play with. We wrote prices on little strips of paper and taped them to the cans. We used Dad's calculator for our cash register. We set our cash register on the old table in the garage. Then we got some play money out of a game in my closet. Sharon made signs that said, "Green Beans: 3 cans for $1.00" and things like that. There were lots of brown paper bags in the kitchen, so we took some to sack the groceries. When our cousins came over, we gave them some play money and let them be the customers. Then we traded places. Who cares if it rains when you are having so much fun?

Follow the directions to illustrate the story.

1. Draw a table and four empty boxes.

2. Draw cans in all the empty boxes.

3. Draw three signs on the wall telling what is being sold.

4. Draw Sharon by the table.

5. Draw some play money in Sharon's hand.

6. Draw two paper sacks under the table.

Scholastic Professional Books

 Write the directions from your house to a another place in your neighborhood. Follow the directions to see if they are correct.

Our Flag

I pledge allegiance to the flag of the United States of America and to the Republic for which it stands, one nation under God, indivisible, with liberty and justice for all.

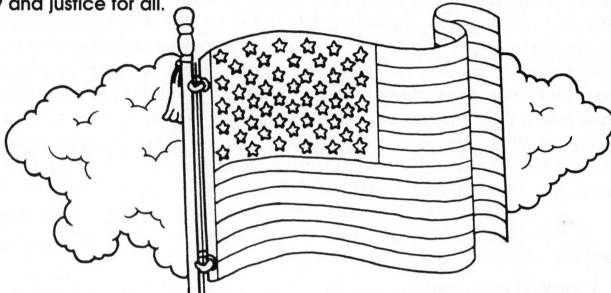

Follow the directions given in each of the following sentences.

1. There is one star for every state in the nation. Count the stars. Write the number in the star.

2. Write the name of your state. _____

3. Color the area around the stars blue. The stars should be white, so do not color them.

4. Write the total number of stripes. _____

5. Seven stripes are red. Beginning with the top stripe, color it and every other stripe red. The six stripes in between should be white, so do not color them.

6. Write these letters in reverse to make two words that tell another name for the flag.   D   L   O   Y   R   O   L   G

   _____   _____

7. Draw a box around every word in the Pledge of Allegiance that has more than six letters.

 Design a flag with four stars and three stripes for a make-believe country. Draw and color it.

After School at Jake's House

*You are **drawing conclusions** when you use your own thoughts to answer the question, "How could that have happened?"*

Jake had a lot of homework to do. It was three pages long. He added and subtracted until his hand got tired of writing.

1. What kind of homework did Jake have?

   spelling   math   reading

   What clues told you the answer? Underline them in the story.

After supper, Jake's dad reminded Jake to do his job. Jake went from room to room unloading baskets and cans into a large plastic bag. Then he took the bag out to the dumpster.

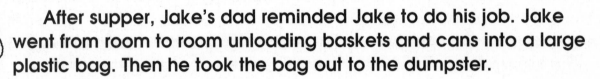

2. What was Jake's job?

   washing dishes   making the bed   taking out the trash

   What clues told you the answer? Underline them in the story.

Now Jake could have some free time. He decided to play "Star Monsters." He turned on the TV and put a cartridge in the player. He watched the monsters fighting on the TV screen while his fingers pushed buttons to make them move.

3. What was Jake doing?

   playing a video game   watching the news   playing with toys

   What clues told you the answer? Underline them in the story.

Jake was tired. He put on his pajamas, brushed his teeth, and crawled under the covers.

4. What was Jake doing?

   waking up   getting ready for school   going to bed

   What clues told you the answer? Underline them in the story.

?ti si tahW

Friday was a special day at my school. First of all, we wore our clothes differently. The back pockets of my jeans were in the front, and my shirt was buttoned up in the back. The teacher began the day with the subject we usually did last. All day, our schedule was opposite of what it usually was. We had to write our name backwards on our papers. At lunch time, we ate dessert first, then our meals! When we went out to recess, we had to walk backward all the way to the playground. Then we had backward relay races. Some people fell down. Everyone was giggling! When it was time to go home, we sang "Good Morning to You."

1. **What special day was it? Circle one.**

   Valentine's Day   Grandparent's Day   Backward Day

2. **Connect the dots in backward ABC order to find out how the principal looked that day.**

$$10 \quad 11$$
$$+3 \quad +3$$

3. **If the math assignment was to count by 5's to 50, how would the children have written it that day? Write the numbers.**

Make up a spelling word list with ten words. Then write them the way the children would have written them on this special day.

They Could Do Better

Read each story below. Choose your answers from the bubble-gum machine. Write them on the lines.

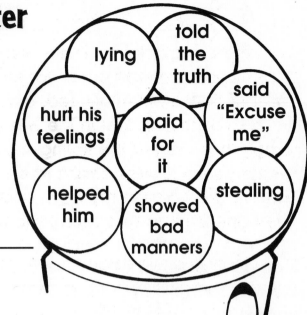

lying

told the truth

said "Excuse me"

hurt his feelings

paid for it

helped him

showed bad manners

stealing

1. **When no one was looking, James took a piece of bubble gum from the candy counter and chewed it. Then he left the store.**

   What was James doing? _____

   What should he have done?

   _____

2. **Dad's boss, Mr. Hill, came for dinner. Zach burped during the meal. He laughed. His dad looked angry.**

   What did Zach do wrong? _____

   What should he have done? _____

3. **While Mom was gone, Ashley played with matches. When Mom came home, she sniffed the air and said, "Ashley, did you light some matches?" Ashley said, "No, Mom, I didn't."**

   What was Ashley doing? _____

   What should she have done? _____

4. **Becky and Cindy saw a boy trip and fall down. Becky pointed at him and told Cindy to look. Then they laughed. The boy looked away sadly.**

   What did Becky and Cindy do? _____

   What should they have done? _____

 On a piece of paper, write the name of a person in your class who has good manners. Explain why you came to that conclusion.

Miss Maple

I am a sugar tree. I live in Vermont. In the summer, my green leaves make a cool, shady place for people to rest. Every fall, my leaves turn brilliant colors of yellow, red, and orange. Some people think it looks like my leaves are on fire! In the winter, my leaves are all gone. I stretch my empty arms out to the falling snow. In the spring, little flowers appear along with my new leaves. That's when the sweet sap inside me begins to rise. People drill holes in my trunk and put a spout in me to drain the sap. Then they boil the sap and make maple syrup!

Add to and color each picture the way it is described in the story.

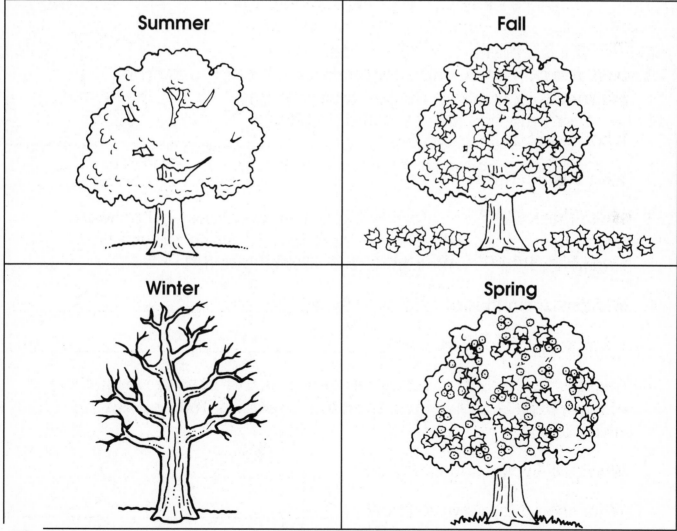

Summer

Fall

Winter

Spring

 Do you like maple syrup? Draw a picture of the kind of food that you would put maple syrup on.

Scholastic Professional Books

Sentence Shapes

Let's have some fun reading and writing sentences! Look at the sentence below. It is shaped like what it is telling about.

Yahoo! I love rollercoasters. They are so much fun! They tickle my tummy!

Now it is your turn! Read each sentence below. Think about what it means. On another piece of paper, rewrite each sentence in the shape that shows what it is telling about. The shapes at the bottom of the page may help you.

1. I wonder if this box has my birthday gift in it.

2. I will send a valentine to someone that I love.

3. Columbus believed that Earth was round.

4. If you see someone without a smile, give them one of yours.

5. Jets taxi down the runway, then fly into the air.

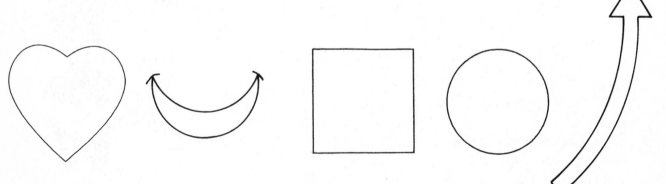

 Now write a shape sentence of your own.

Summer Vacation

 Grouping like things together helps you see how parts of a story are connected and makes the story easier to understand.

Last summer, Dad, Mom, Tim, and Tara went to the beach in Florida. They swam, fished, built sandcastles, and went sailing. Mom brought a picnic lunch. She spread a blanket on the sand and set out ham sandwiches, potato chips, apples, and cookies. She brought lemonade in the cooler. Later, Tim and Tara walked along the beach and saw a crab walking sideways. A stray dog was barking at it. A starfish had washed up on the beach, too. Tim threw bread crumbs up in the air to feed a flock of seagulls. Then the family went back to the hotel, and Tim and Tara played video games until bedtime.

Use the story to find the answers. Fill in the blanks.

Picnic Items

_____

_____

_____

_____

_____

People Who Went to the Beach

_____

_____

_____

What They Did

_____

_____

_____

_____

Living Things They Saw on the Beach

_____

_____

_____

_____

On a piece of paper, make one list of things you would take for a day at the beach and another list of what you would take for a day in the mountains.

Which One Doesn't Belong?

 Look for similarities when grouping items.

Read each list. Cross out the word that doesn't belong. Then choose a word from the kite that belongs with each list and write it in the blank.

1. grouchy   mad   cheerful   fussy   _____

2. north   away   east   south   _____

3. goat   blue jay robin   eagle   _____

4. juice   milk   tea   mud   _____

5. hand   toy   foot   head   _____

6. David   Bob   Ronald   Sarah   _____

7. spinach   cake   cookies   pie   _____

8. glue   bicycle pencils   scissors _____

9. penny   nickel   quarter   marble   _____

On the kite:
arm
dime
George
pudding
lemonade
parakeet
crayons
angry
west

Now read these categories. In each box, write the number from the above list that matches the category.

Birds	Desserts	Bad Feelings
Boys' Names	Money	School Supplies
Directions	Body Parts	Drinks

 Write a list of five things that go with this category: Things That Are Hot.

My Favorites

This page is all about you! Read the categories and write your own answers.

My Favorite TV Shows	My Favorite Foods	My Favorite Sports
_____	_____	_____
_____	_____	_____
_____	_____	_____

Draw two of your favorite people here and write their names.

Favorite Thing to Do After School

_____

Favorite Thing to Do With My Family

_____

Favorite Color

_____

Favorite Holiday

_____

Favorite Song

_____

Favorite Movie

_____

Favorite School Subject

_____

Trade pages with friends and read what they wrote. You might get to know them a little better!

Will He Be All Right?

Use story details to guess what will happen next.

Father Eagle said to his young son, "Today is a very special day. You will fly for the first time." Baby Eagle was afraid. He said, "But Father, I don't know how. What should I do?" His father laid a strong wing on his little shoulder and said, "You will know." They stood at the edge of a very high cliff. Far below were huge rocks and a canyon. "Ride the wind, my son!" said Father Eagle, and he gently pushed his son off the cliff. Baby Eagle yelled, "Help! Help!" and wildly flapped his wings. All of a sudden something wonderful happened!

Help!

He fell on the rocks.

He got hurt.

He broke his wing on a tree limb.

He learned to fly.

1. What do you think happened next? Color the rock that tells the most likely answer.

2. Why did you choose that answer? Find the sentence in the story that gives you a hint that the story has a happy ending. Write it here.

_____

_____

Unscramble the words and write the answer: **ODPRU**   **AARDFI**

3. How do you think Baby Eagle felt at first when he was pushed off the cliff? _____

4. How do you think Father Eagle felt at the end of the story? _____

What Will Happen Next?

Read each story. Write your answer on the blanks.

1. The baseball game was tied 6-6 at the bottom of the ninth inning with bases loaded. The home team batter hit a high fly ball deep into right field. The outfielder caught the ball but then dropped it. What will happen next?

_____

_____

2. Latoya decided to bake some brownies. She put them in the oven and went outside and jumped in the pool. She swam for a long time. She forgot all about the brownies. What will happen next?

_____

_____

3. Mrs. Lopez ran over a big nail. It stuck in the tire. Air began to seep out. What will happen next?

_____

_____

4. The wind began to blow. Dark clouds drifted in. Lightning cracked, and thunder roared. What will happen next?

_____

_____

5. One day Greg left his toy truck on the stairs. Mom came down the stairs carrying a laundry basket, piled high with dirty towels. She stepped on Greg's truck. What will happen next?

_____

_____

6. Dad and Sam went fishing. They rowed the boat to the middle of the lake. Then they hit a rock that made a hole in the boat. Water started rushing in it. What will happen next?

_____

_____

 Choose one of the stories above and draw a picture of what happens next.

Wishes Come True

Once upon a time Rita Rabbit was complaining to Diana Duck. "You always have fun, swimming around in the lake. I wish I was a duck. You're lucky." Diana Duck said, "Oh, really? Well, I wish I was a rabbit! You can hop so fast and go so far. I think you're lucky!" Just then the Good Fairy appeared and said, "You are both lucky! I will grant you each your wish." All of a sudden Rita Rabbit became a duck! She waddled to the lake and went for a swim. Diana Duck became a rabbit and hopped down the road as fast as she could go. At the end of the day, Rita was wet and cold. She missed her family. She missed her home in the hole at the bottom of the hollow tree. She wanted to hop over there, but it was too far, and all she could do was waddle. Diana was having trouble, too. She had hopped so far away that she got lost. She began to cry. She wanted to go home to the lake. Just then . . . POOF! The Good Fairy appeared again. She granted Rita and Diana one more wish.

Draw what you think happened when Rita got her second wish.

Draw what you think happened when Diana got her second wish.

 If you had a wish, what would it be? On a piece of paper, draw a picture of what might happen if your wish came true.

Zoo Reports

 Compare *means to look for things that are the same.*
Contrast *means to look for things that are different.*

The second-grade class went to the zoo for a field trip. The next day, the teacher asked the children to write a report about what they learned. Read the two reports below.

Ryan	Jessica
What I Learned at the Zoo	**What I Learned at the Zoo**
I learned about the giant tortoise. It was so big that the guide let us sit on its back. Some tortoises live to be over 100 years old! That's older than my grandpa!	The tallest animal on earth is the giraffe. It eats leaves from the tops of the trees. Giraffes come from Africa.
The slowest-moving mammal is the three-toed sloth. It hangs from trees and eats fruit. Some sloths sleep more than 20 hours a day. What a lazy animal!	I learned about an albino alligator. It was white instead of green. The guide told us that it was born without the coloring of other alligators.
I thought the albino alligator was really cool. It wasn't green. It was completely white all over. It was born that way.	I saw an owl sleeping in a tree. Owls sleep in the daytime and hunt at night. When they sleep, they don't fall out of the tree because they have sharp claws that lock onto the branch.

Ryan and Jessica each wrote about three animals. Write the names of the animals they wrote about in the correct circles. In the center where both circles overlap, write the name of the animal that they both wrote about.

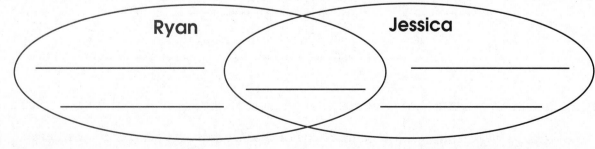

 Write three facts about a zoo animal. If you need help, use a dictionary or encyclopedia.

Scholastic Professional Books

The Contest

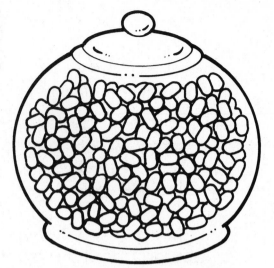

The Super Grocery Store held a contest. Whoever could guess the correct number of jelly beans in the big jar would win a prize. There were exactly 372 jelly beans. Two people guessed the right answer. They were Joey Jumpjolly and Harry Honkhorn. Since there were two winners, both of them were given a $20 gift certificate. Joey Jumpjolly decided to spend his prize money on his favorite foods. He bought vanilla ice cream, animal cookies, angel food cake, and a chocolate candy bar. Harry Honkhorn had a different idea. He used his money to buy bacon, eggs, cereal, and waffles.

How are Joey and Harry alike? How are they different? To find out, work the puzzle below. Cross out all the Q's, V's, Z's, and X's. Next cross out all the numbers 1–9. Then cross out every question mark. What is left? Write the words in order in the blanks at the bottom of the page.

```
3  ?  5  Q  B  O  T  H  9  9  7  X  H  A  D  6  2
T  W  E  N  T  Y  X  Q  8  D  O  L  L  A  R  S  7
X  V  5  Z  T  O  4  ?  Q  S  P  E  N  D  3  2  1
?  Q  J  O  E  Y  3  B  O  U  G  H  T  Z  V  7  6
Z  9  X  S  W  E  E  T  S  4  ?  V  H  A  R  R  Y
7  ?  V  Z  V  B  O  U  G  H  T  8  9  X  V  3  7
B  R  E  A  K  F  A  S  T  4  ?  V  F  O  O  D  X
```

_____ _____ _____ _____ _____

_____ _____. _____ _____ _____

_____. _____ _____ _____

_____.

💡 On a piece of paper, make a list of what you would buy at a grocery store. Are your choices more like Joey's or Harry's?

The Accident

Kendra and her mom left their house on Oak Street to go to school. Kendra put on her safety belt. About that same time, Lacey and her mom left their house on Maple Street. On the way to school, Lacey bounced up and down on the seat watching her pigtails fly up and down in the mirror. She had forgotten to wear her safety belt. Both moms turned into the school parking lot at the same time, and they crashed into each other! Kendra was not hurt. Her safety belt kept her in her seat. But, Lacey fell forward and bumped her head HARD! She cried and cried. She had to go to the hospital and get an X ray. Lacey got well in a day or two, but she learned an important lesson!

Draw a 🙂 in the correct column.

	Kendra	Lacey	both
driven to school by Mom			
wore a safety belt			
didn't wear a safety belt			
lives on Maple Street			
was in a wreck			
bumped her head			
got an X ray			
lives on Oak Street			
bounced up and down in the car			
didn't get hurt			
learned a lesson			

 Write a sentence telling why it is important to wear a safety belt.

What Is Cotton?

Cotton is a very useful plant. Farmers plant cotton in the spring. The plants grow and make white <u>flowers</u>. When a flower falls off, a <u>boll</u> grows in its place. The boll is the seed pod, which looks kind of like a walnut. When the boll dries, it splits open. Inside is the fluffy, white cotton. Farmers take the cotton to a <u>gin</u>. Machines at the gin take the cotton out of the bolls. The cotton is pressed into wrapped bundles called <u>bales</u>. The bales are sent to cotton mills where the cotton is spun into <u>yarn</u>. The yarn is woven into <u>fabric</u>, or cloth. Then it is made into clothes, sheets, curtains, towels, and many other things.

Draw a line from the word to its picture. The story will help you.

flowers •

boll •

gin •

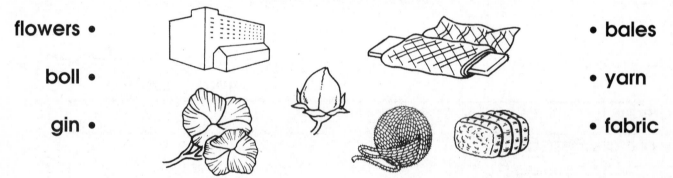

• bales

• yarn

• fabric

Color the things below that could be made from cotton. Put an X on things that are not made of cotton.

Draw and color the clothes that you are wearing today. Put an X on the ones made of cotton.

Busy as a Bee

Bees are hardworking insects. They live together in a nest called a <u>hive</u>. There is one <u>queen bee</u> in each hive. She is the largest bee. There are hundreds of <u>worker bees</u>. The worker bees fly from flower to flower gathering a sweet liquid called <u>nectar</u>. They make honey from the nectar and store it in little rooms in the hive. Each little room is a <u>cell</u>. Many cells in a row make a <u>honeycomb</u>. When a bear or a person tries to steal the honey, the bees swarm, flying around in large groups. Each bee has a <u>stinger</u> to protect it from its enemies. A person who is a <u>beekeeper</u> makes wooden hives for bees, then sells the honey when the bees finish making it.

Look at the picture below. Use each underlined word in the story to label the pictures.

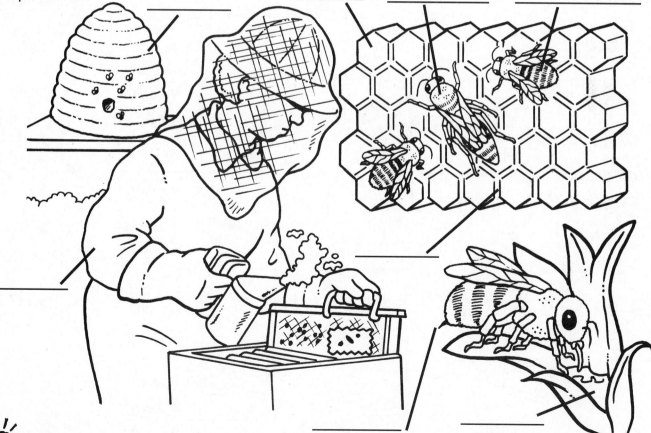

On a piece of paper, make a list of five other insects. You may need an encyclopedia to help you.

Sioux Life

Many years ago, the Sioux tribes lived on the grasslands, called the <u>plains</u>. They killed bison for meat. Some called these animals <u>buffalo</u>. The Sioux cut the meat in strips and dried it in the sun to make <u>jerky</u>. Buffalo hides were used to make <u>tepees</u>. The hides were wrapped around long poles, making tall tents. The tepees could be taken down and moved around from place to place to follow the buffalo herds. <u>Canoes</u> were used for traveling down a river or crossing a lake. The Sioux made <u>buckskin clothing</u> out of deer hides. Sometimes they decorated their clothes with colorful beads. A group of Sioux living together was called a tribe. The leader of the tribe was called the <u>chief</u>. The chief often wore a long <u>headdress</u> of eagle feathers.

Draw a line from each word to the picture that matches it.

- plains
- buffalo
- jerky
- tepee
- canoe
- buckskin clothing
- chief
- headdress

Circle the things below that the Sioux tribes might have had. Put an X on the things they didn't have.

Name _____

Chain Reaction

 *In a story, there is usually a reason something happens. This is the **cause**. What happened as a result is the **effect**.*

It was a long way to Aunt Ruth's house. Terry and Mary Beth started getting a little bit too loud in the back seat, so Dad said, "Girls, settle down. Be quiet and read your books." They knew Dad meant business. Just then, Mary Beth saw a bee flying around in the car. Her eyes got big, and she ducked her head, swatting the bee away. Terry looked at her, and Mary Beth loudly whispered, "BEEEE!" Terry wanted to scream, but she knew Dad would get mad. "What are you two doing back there?" Dad asked. Just then, the bee landed on Dad's bald head. Mary Beth knew she had to save him from getting stung, so she whopped Dad on the head with her book. Dad jerked the steering wheel, and the car ran off the road and through a fence. The cows that were in the field ran away. Later, a police officer gave Dad a ticket for reckless driving.

Draw a line to match the cause to the effect.

The girls got too loud, so

The girls saw a bee land on Dad's bald head, so

The car ran off the road and through a fence

which let the cows out.

Dad said to be quiet.

Mary Beth whopped Dad on the head with a book.

Keep the chain going! Write what happened next because Dad ran off the road.

An American Volcano

Mount Saint Helens is an active volcano in the state of Washington. In 1980, this volcano erupted, spewing hot lava into the air. Explosions caused a huge cloud of dust. This gray dust filled the air and settled on houses and cars many miles away. The thick dust made it hard for people and animals to breathe. The explosions flattened trees on the side of the mountain. The hot rocks caused forest fires. The snow that was on the mountain melted quickly, causing floods and mud slides. Mount Saint Helens still erupts from time to time but not as badly as it did in 1980.

Read each phrase below. Write the number of each phrase in the explosion of the volcano that correctly completes the sentence.

1. **Mount Saint Helens erupted,**

2. **The thick ash made it hard**

3. **The explosions**

4. **The hot rocks caused**

5. **Melting snow caused**

6. **Because Mount Saint Helens is an active volcano,**

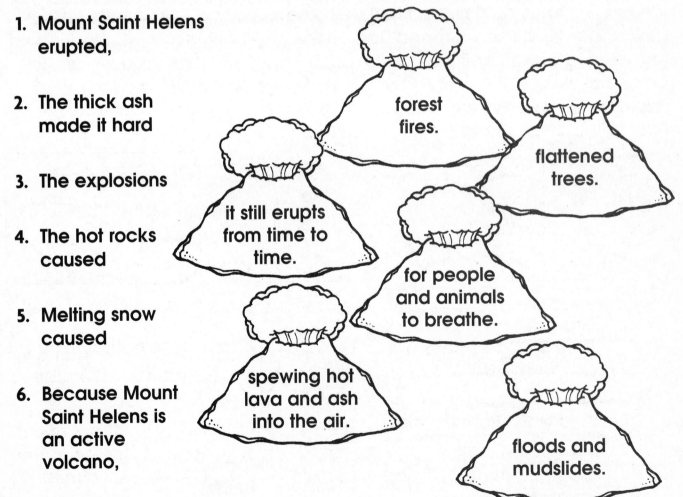

forest fires.

flattened trees.

it still erupts from time to time.

for people and animals to breathe.

spewing hot lava and ash into the air.

floods and mudslides.

Write a story that begins this way:
We were camping in the mountains, when all of a sudden a volcano erupted!

My Favorite Dentist

A **character** *is a person or animal in a story. To understand a character better, you should pay attention to the details a story often gives about the character.*

Some kids are scared to go to the dentist, but not me. I have a funny dentist. His name is Dr. Smileyface. I don't think that's his real name, but that's what he tells all the kids who come to see him. He has a cool waiting room. It has video games and a big toy box. Dr. Smileyface always wears funny hats. Sometimes he has his face painted. He asks funny questions like "Are you married yet?" and "Do you eat flowers to make your breath smell so sweet?" That makes me laugh. One time, he told me this joke, "What has lots of teeth but never goes to the dentist? A comb!" When I laughed, he pulled my tooth. It didn't hurt at all! He also teaches me how to take care of my teeth because he says he doesn't want me to get a cavity the size of the Grand Canyon. Before I go home, he always gives me a surprise. Last time I went, he gave me a rubber spider to scare my mom with!

Color the pictures that could be Dr. Smileyface. Put an X on the pictures that could not not be him.

Draw a line from the toothbrush to the tooth that makes the sentence true.

6. Dr. Smileyface makes

7. The child who wrote this story

8. Dr. Smileyface teaches kids

9. Dr. Smileyface sends kids home

how to take care of their teeth.

his patients laugh.

with a surprise.

is not afraid to go to the dentist.

What a Kid!

Tad is a very special boy. He is confined to a wheelchair. He was born with a disease that made him unable to walk. Some boys would be sad or angry about that, but not Tad. Instead, he looks for ways to make people happy. He called the Green Oaks School for the Blind and asked if he could volunteer. They said, "Sure!" Tad went to the school and quickly made friends. Every day, he reads books to the children. He plays games with them. Sometimes he helps them do their schoolwork. The children at the school nicknamed him Lucky because they feel so lucky to have him as a friend. That makes Tad very happy!

- If Tad is confined to a wheelchair, write an H in Box 1 and Box 9. If not, write a J in both boxes.

- If Tad feels sorry for himself, write a U in Box 2 and Box 10. If he doesn't, write a E in both boxes.

- If Tad looks for ways to make people happy, write an L in Box 3. If he doesn't, write a B.

- If Tad volunteers at the River Oak School for the Blind, write a Z in Box 4. If that is not correct, write a P.

- If Tad reads to the blind children, write an N in Box 5. If not, write a V.

- If Tad plays games with the blind children, write a G in Box 6. If not, write a D.

- If Tad helps them with their homework, write an O in Box 7. If not, write an R.

- If the children nicknamed Tad "Grumpy," write a K in Box 8. If not, write a T.

- If Tad is a happy person, write an R in Box 11. If not, write a C.

This is the story of Helen Keller.

Tad's secret of happiness is

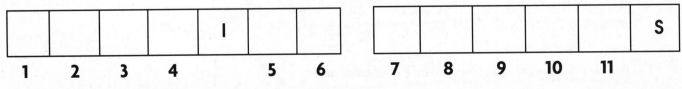

1	2	3	4		5	6		7	8	9	10	11
			I								S

Lunch Lady

by Karen Jackson

I don't know her name. She is one of the workers in our school cafeteria. I just call her Lunch Lady. She's my friend. There are several nice ladies in the cafeteria, but the Lunch Lady is the nicest of all. Every day she smiles at me when I go through the line. She says things like, "Hi Karen! Are you having a good day?" Lunch Lady always remembers that I like chicken nuggets the best. Whenever that is what is being served, she hands me the chicken nuggets and says, "Look, your favorite!" One day, I tripped and dropped my tray. Food went all over the floor. I was so embarrassed, but Lunch Lady came to my rescue. She helped me pick up the mess, and she told me, "Don't worry about it. It's okay." That made me feel better. Another time, I was at the shoe store with my mom, and I saw Lunch Lady. She gave me a big hug. The reason I admire Lunch Lady is because she is friendly and kind.

Read each sentence. Find the words that are wrong and cross them out. Then above them write the correct word or words that make the sentence true.

1. Karen wrote about Lunch Man.

2. Karen's favorite food is hot dogs.

3. Lunch Lady frowns when Karen comes through the line.

4. When Karen dropped her tray, Miss Daniels helped her.

5. One time, Karen saw the Lunch Lady at the hardware store.

6. Karen admires Lunch Lady because she is friendly and m[ ]

 Write a paragraph about someone you admire.

Limericks

 A **limerick** is a poem that has five lines in it. It is usually funny and has a special order of rhyming words. The first two lines rhyme. Then the next two lines rhyme. Then the last line rhymes with the first two lines. Read the limerick below.

There once was a fellow named Jed

Who spent too much time in his bed.

He slept for so long

That something went wrong,

His hair grew long on his head.

In the limerick above, draw a red circle around the three words that rhyme. Draw a green box around the two words that rhyme.

Help finish the limerick below by filling in the blanks with a word from the Word Bank.

Word Bank
class   lazy   pass   crazy   Daisy

There once was a student named __ __ __ __ __

Who wouldn't work because she was __ __ __ __ .

She slept during __ __ __ __ __ .

No way she could __ __ __ __ .

Her poor teacher finally went __ __ __ __ __ .

 Work with a partner and write a limerick. It helps to start with three rhyming words and two other rhyming words, then make up the sentences.

Scholastic Professional Books

A Tall Tale

 A **tall tale** is a story about a superhuman hero. The story is funny because everything is exaggerated. That means it is much bigger and better than real life. Read the tall tale below. Use a yellow crayon or marker to highlight each thing that is exaggerated.

Paul Bunyan

Paul Bunyan was a mighty man. He was so big, he had to use wagon wheels for buttons. Paul was a lumberjack. He owned a blue ox named Babe. Paul and Babe were so big that their tracks made 10,000 lakes in the state of Minnesota.

Paul worked with seven axmen. They were so big that they were six feet tall sitting down. All of them were named Elmer. So when Paul called "Elmer!" they all came running.

The year of the two winters, it got so cold that when the axmen would speak, their words froze in midair. When it thawed in the spring, there was a terrible chatter for weeks.

One time Paul caught two giant mosquitoes and used them to drill holes in maple trees.

Paul Bunyan had a purple cow named Lucy. In the year of two winters, it got so cold that Lucy's milk turned to ice cream before it hit the pail.

The End

 Choose two funny sentences above and copy them on another piece of paper. Then draw a picture about each one.

A Play

*A **play** is a story written as a script. Actors read the script, then memorize their lines, so they can pretend to be the characters in the story. Read the play below. The words in parentheses tell the actors what to do.*

A Bad Idea

(Megan and Kyle are talking before class starts.)

Megan: Hey, Kyle, are you ready for the big test today? I studied that list of words and the definitions for two hours last night.

Kyle: Oh, brother! I didn't study at all. I just wrote all the answers on the palm of my hand, see?

Megan: Kyle! You can't do that! That's cheating!

Kyle: Hey, don't worry. I won't get caught. Mrs. King will never know. *(Teacher passes out the tests.)*

Mrs. King: Okay, no more talking. Everyone keep your eyes on your own paper, and cover your answers with a cover sheet. You may begin. *(Kyle looks at his hand when the teacher isn't looking.)*

Joe: *(raising his hand)* Mrs. King, may I get a drink? I have the hiccups.

Mrs. King: Yes, you may.

Kyle: *(raising his hand)* Mrs. King, may I get a drink, too?

Mrs. King: Kyle, what is that on your hand? I think you better come to my desk.

Kyle: *(looks over at Megan)* Oh no . . .

Megan: Busted!

Use markers or crayons to follow each direction.

1. The words in parentheses are called *stage directions*. Underline all the stage directions with a blue line.

2. Highlight Megan's words in pink.

3. Highlight Kyle's words in yellow.

4. Highlight Mrs. King's words in green.

5. Highlight Joe's words in orange.

Page 4
1. spots; My domino has two white spots, and yours has five. 2. sea bird; A gray seabird flew by the cruise ship. 3. A green stone; The queen had a beautiful necklace made of a green stone. 4. flute player; My sister is the best flute player in the high school band.

Page 5
Neil Armstrong was the first man to walk on the moon.

Page 6
1. IOU; 2. EZ; 3. ICU; 4. AB; 5. TP; 6. MT; 7. IV

Page 7
Police officers help people.

Page 8
On Saturday, Rachel got up early. Mom was still asleep, so Rachel made her own breakfast. She put some peanut butter in a bowl She mixed it with a little *honey. Then she stirred in some *oatmeal, *bran flakes, and *raisins. It tasted yummy! When Mom got up, she said, "Oh, You made granola!"

Page 9
1. B; 2. U; 3. L; 4. L; 5. R ; 6. I; 7. D; 8. E; 9. R; 10. S; Bullriders

Page 10

Page 11
Make-believe: pig, goat and sheep, horses, pizza and hamburgers, mouse and table, golden eggs, crickets (The others are real.)

Page 12
Real: a woman feeding animals; a grandmother living alone; sleeping on hay in a barn; a house burning down; crying that her house burned (The rest are make-believe.)

Page 13
Children's answers will vary.

Page 14
1. Mia begged Spooky to come down. 2. Mia asked Mr. Carson for help. 3. Mr. Carson called his firefighter friends. 4. The fire truck came. 5. A firefighter climbed the ladder. 6. Spooky jumped to a tree and climbed down. 7. Mia scolded Spooky. 8. The firefighters laughed.

Page 15
Writing; Math; Recess; Social Studies; 11:00; Story Time; Science; Spelling; Music

Page 16
3, 1, 4, 2, 6, 7, 5, 8

Page 17
(Child's name) knows how to follow directions!

Page 18
Check child's picture.

Page 19
1. 50; 2. (your state); 4. 13; 6. Old Glory; 7. allegiance, America, Republic, indivisible, liberty, justice

Page 20
1. math; 2. taking out the trash; 3. playing a video game; 4. going to bed

Page 21
1. Backward Day
2. Check child's dot-to-dot picture.
3. 50, 45, 40, 35, 30, 25, 20, 15, 10, 5

Page 22
1. stealing; paid for it; 2. showed bad manners; said "Excuse me"; 3. lying; told the truth; 4. hurt his feelings; helped him

Page 23
Each tree should be illustrated as described in the story.

Page 24
1. box shape; 2. heart shape; 3. circle shape; 4. semi-circle shape; 5. arc shape

Page 25
1. Zolak's shadow; 2. No; 3. No; He didn't see any real earthling, only his own shadow.

4.

Page 26
1, 4, 6, 7, 10, 11, 14, 15, 18, 20, 21, 24, 26, teapot

Page 27
People Who Went to the Beach: Dad, Mom, Tim, and Tara

What They Did: swam, fished, built sandcastles, went sailing

Picnic Items: ham sandwiches, potato chips, apples, cookies, lemonade

Living Things They Saw on the Beach: crab, dog, starfish, sea gulls

Page 28
1. cheerful; angry; 2. away; west; 3. goat; parakeet; 4. mud; lemonade; 5. toy; arm; 6. Sarah; George; 7. spinach; pudding; 8. bicycle; crayon; 9. marble; dime

Binds 3; Desserts 7; Bad Feelings 1; Boys' Names 6; Money 9; School Supplies 8; Directions 2; Body Parts 5; Drinks 4

Page 29
Children's answers will vary.

Scholastic Professional Books

Page 30

1. He learned to fly. 2. All of a sudden something wonderful happened. 3. afraid; 4. proud

Page 31

(Accept any reasonable answers.)

1. The home team wins the game. 2. The brownies will burn. 3. She will have a flat tire. 4. It will rain. 5. Mom will fall. 6. The boat will sink.

Page 32

Children should draw pictures that show these conclusions: Rita became a rabbit again. Diana became a duck again.

Page 33

Ryan—giant tortoise, 3-toed sloth

Both—albino alligator

Jessica—giraffe, owl

Page 34

Both had twenty dollars to spend. Joey bought sweets. Harry bought breakfast food.

Page 35

both, Kendra, Lacey, Lacey, both, Lacey, Lacey, Kendra, Lacey, Kendra, Lacey

Page 36

flowers, boll, gin, bales, yarn, fabric

Things made of cotton: shirt, pillow, sock, shorts, towel.

not made of cotton: scissors, pitcher, trumpet, cake

Page 37

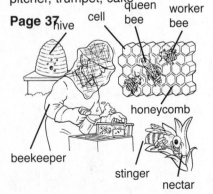

hive, cell, queen bee, worker bee, honeycomb, beekeeper, stinger, nectar

Page 38

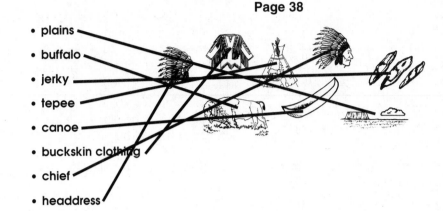

- plains
- buffalo
- jerky
- tepee
- canoe
- buckskin clothing
- chief
- headdress

Children should put an X on the pictures of the computer, the helicopter, and the car. Other pictures should be circled.

Page 39

The girls got too loud, so Dad said to be quiet. The girls saw a bee land on Dad's bald head, so Mary Beth whopped Dad on the head with a book. The car ran off the road and through a fence, which let the cows out.

Page 40

1. spewing hot lava and ash into the air; 2. for people and animals to breathe; 3. flattened trees; 4. forest fires; 5. floods and mudslides; 6. it still erupts from time to time

Page 41

1, 2

6. Dr. Smileyface makes his patients laugh. 7. The child who wrote this story is not afraid to go to the dentist. 8. Dr. Smileyface teaches kids how to take care of their teeth. 9. Dr. Smileyface sends kids home with a surprise.

Page 42

HELPING OTHERS

Page 43

1. ~~Man~~; Lady; 2. ~~hot dogs~~; chicken nuggets; 3. ~~frowns~~; smiles; 4. ~~Miss Daniels~~; Lunch Lady; 5. ~~hardware~~; shoe; 6. ~~mean~~; kind